# I Like Likeable Things

## Author

Fannie Lewis Barnes

This book is the property of:

To: _____

From: _____

Date: _____

Message:

Copyright - Fannie Lewis Barnes

ISBN - 9781737657163

Printed - United States of America

## Graphics

The pictures used in this book are from the free content vector clip art website:

www.openclipart.org

Special thanks to

support@openclipart.org

for giving me permission to use their wonderful website/clip art in order to enhance this book for children's enjoyment.

Recognition to DeMorris and LaWanda Burrell of SUSUEntertainmentLLC for their assistance with this reader.

# R E A D

**R**elax
**E**njoy
**A**nd
**D**evelop

# R E A D

Relax with this little book
Enjoy it from the shelf,
And you will see that you can
Develop skills all by yourself!


Ready to hear of some things
Each child likes to do?
After you complete this book
Decide if you like them too.

## Words to Know

likeable

fruit

silk

veggies

music

ice cream

soccer

dolphin

basketball

microphone

These are some things that I like to do,

maybe you like some of these things too.

# I like to read,

I like to sing,

I like a lot of likeable things.

I like eating fruit,

I like drinking milk,

I like this bag made of silk.

I like eating veggies,

I like eating ice cream,

do you like these
likeable things?

# I like playing music,

I like hearing
birds sing,

I like a lot of
likeable things.

I like video games,

I like these lights
on a string,

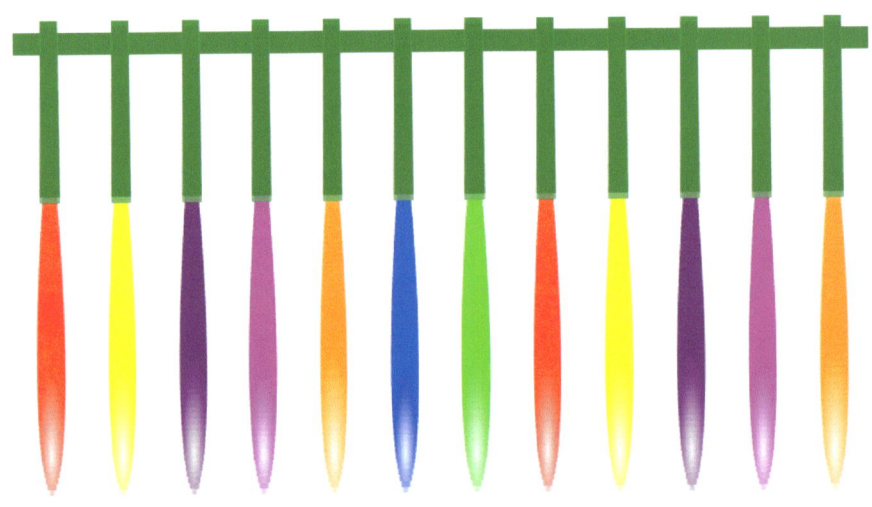

I like all of these

likeable things.

I like playing soccer,

I like riding my bike,

do you like these
likeable things
that I like?

I like playing
with my dog,

I like watching
dolphin "Blue,"

what are some
likeable things
that you like to do?

I like playing this game
with my friend,

It does not matter who loses
or who wins.

I like learning
in school,

I like
movies in 3-D,

All of these likeable things are fun to me!

I like playing in leaves sometimes in the fall;

I like playing this sport, what is this? A basketball!

I like painting with colors,
red, blue, yellow and green,

Do you like painting different likeable things?

I like some trees that are short,
I like some that are tall,

Do you like any of these trees at all?

Reading and learning can be likeable things too,
Here are some other likeable skills for you.
Some likeable things are really good you know,
These practical worksheets can be likeable also.

Color with friends or if you are alone, start by coloring this microphone.

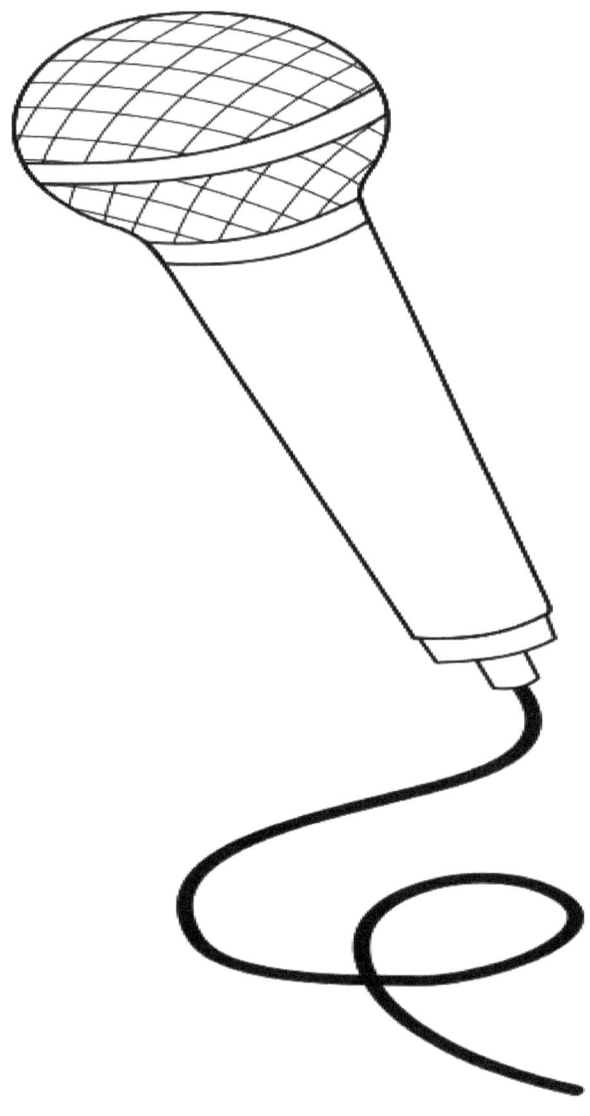

# Color likeable things that some people eat,

Do you think these likeable things are a treat?

Some likeable things are different, I realize
but, I think everyone like these likeable fries!

I like likeable things that I can cook,
I hope you like this, "I Like Likeable Things book!"

I like when you learn
I like when you read,
I like when you see
that there is a need!
Review what you have learned
this is not a test,
Which of these likeable
activities do you like best?

# Draw lines to connect the same words.

| | |
|---|---|
| likeable | veggies |
| fruit | ice cream |
| silk | microphone |
| veggies | soccer |
| music | likeable |
| ice cream | dolphin |
| soccer | basketball |
| dolphin | music |
| basketball | silk |
| microphone | fruit |

# Write in the correct missing letters.

likeable      l __ __ e a __ __ e

fruit         f r __ i __

silk          s __ __ k

veggies       v __ g __ i e __

music         m u __ i __

ice cream     i __ e   c r __ __ m

soccer        s o __ c __ __

dolphin       d o l __ __ i n

basketball    b __ s __ e t __ a __ l

microphone    m i __ r __ p h __ n __

## Write the words in ABC order.

likeable         _____

fruit            _____

silk             _____

veggies          _____

music            _____

ice cream        _____

soccer           _____

dolphin          _____

basketball       _____

microphone       _____

# Skill Suggestions

Listed below are a few suggestions to use upon completion of this story. Incorporate these and other suggestions according to the learner's functioning abilities.

1. Ask learner the title of this book.
2. Ask learner the initials or name of the author.
3. Ask learner to name some of the likeable things listed in the story.
4. Ask learner to name likeable thing (s) listed on specific page (s).
5. Ask learner to name the veggies on p. 7.
6. Ask learner what items are on the string?
7. Ask learner, what is the color/name of the dolphin? (p.16)
8. Ask learner, what does the boy like to do who is holding the book?
9. Have learner to name likeable things that he or she likes to do.
10. Have learner point to, repeat specified words in this story or re-read story.

## Author's Information

Email:  morepsplease@gmail.com

Face Book:  Fannie Lewis Barnes

Amazon.com:  Books by Fannie Lewis Barnes

Published books on Amazon are:

~ <u>I Must Read</u> - Curriculum/Common Core Standards Based Material, (Alphabets A-Z, pictures, long/short vowels, simple sentences, instructions)

~ <u>Reading As I Learn</u> (R.A.I.L.) – Counting 1-10, number words, colors, color words, pictures

~ <u>Ray and Mae</u> (bringing smiles) – Best Bunny Buddies making everyone and everything happy with their presence

~ <u>My Little Friends</u> – (Different baby animals)

~ <u>Let's Stick Together</u> – (Friends sticking together)

~ <u>Once Upon A Time</u>- (A story about talking insects)

*Books include Skilful Suggestions and Worksheets

www.ingramcontent.com/pod-product-compliance
Lightning Source LLC
Chambersburg PA
CBHW042123040426

42450CB00002B/52